SEGOVIA'S FINGERNAIL

By

LEE PENNINGTON

ARTERIAL POETRY

Arterial Poetry
Goshen, KY

www.arterialpoetry.com

Segovia's Fingernail

Copyright © 2019 by Lee Pennington

First Edition

ISBN: **978-1-937979-75-1**

Back Cover Photo by Brenda Shake Osmon

All rights reserved

No part of this book may be reproduced in any form or by any electronic or mechanical means, including information storage and retrieval systems, without written permission from the author, except for the use of brief quotations in a book review.

DEDICATION

*For Lonnie and Roberta Brown
with deep appreciation
for their friendship*

ACKNOWLEDGEMENTS

The author wishes to thank the following publications where certain of these poems first appeared: *The Spirit of '76, Poet* (India), *Olè, The Idler, Promising Poets of the Midwest, Poetry Prevue, Pegasus, Arena, The Angels, American Weave, The Saint, Midnight, South & West, Bay Shore Breeze, Wind, Hoosier Challenger, Cardinal Poetry Quarterly, Flame Annual, Mountain Review, Approaches, Experiment, Free Lance,* and *Louisville Gazette.*

TABLE OF CONTENTS

DEDICATION

ACKNOWLEDGEMENTS

ILLUSTRATIONS BY JILL BAKER

PART 1

COUNTING GALAXIES 1

- SEGOVIA'S FINGERNAIL 3
- MUSIC'S SPHERE...5
- POET LAYERS...6
- STANDING ON THE BANKS OF THE HUDSON................8
- LATE SHOWS 12
- SHADOWS UNDER THE STONE 14
- AMARETTO KISSES..17
- THE WALLS SING...18

PART 2

MOSTLY A SHADOW..21

- DRAWING WATER 22
- THE HEART OF DOGHOWLS..24
- THIS MORNING I WAS THIRTY 25
- FREEFALL RAIN 28
- NIGHT THEY CALL IT..29
- TO FILL AN EMPTY LOCKET...30
- DOWN IN THE DUMP..32
- ALPHABETICAL 34
- I AM LOVED WITH SLABS OF SUNBURN 36

    THE MAGICIAN'S REPLY 37
    REVERSE 38
    BETWEEN THE STARS AND TREES 39
    TIME'S VACANT PITS 40

PART 3
STOLEN SEEDS 41
    ASCENSION 42
    PAGAN GODS 43
    MODERN GALILEE 44
    DISCIPLE DOVES 45
    ROLLING SILENCE 46
    4TH STREET 47
    CREATION 48
    PARADOX 50
    WILDWOOD 51
    DAY LIGHT 52
    FISH SONGS 53
    IN DARKNESS 54

PART 4 57
THE GREAT DARK PLACES 57
    IN THIS THE WORLD 58
    BAREFOOT WITHOUT THE GULLS 59
    RAW BACKWARDS 60
    "WAR IS KIND" 61
    FLY BY NIGHT 62
    THEY AND THEIR FATHERS 64

POLLUTION 66

PART 5

COINS ON THE EYES 67
    ON A BIRD CRASHING INTO A CLOSED WINDOW 68
    BLUE GILLS 70
    HAITI REVISITED 72
    LIST OF THE DEAD 81
    FAR CRY FROM ENEMY 82

PART 6

MUSIC OF FUR 83
    THE SEA OF MY FINGERS 84
    THE WHITE WOLF OF YOUR EYES 85
    LEDA'S BIRD 86
    APHRODITE WELCOMES NIGHT 89
    PERFECT CIRCLES 90
    CLINGING TO SEAWEEDS 92
    EVEN THEN 93
    SILENT FISH 95
    THE HOMELY GOLD HAIR GIRL AT THE FOOT OF THE STAIR 96
    THE BLUE GIRL 97
    NO GOLF PERMITTED HERE 98
    BURDEN 99
    THE RAIN WOMAN WALKS 100

PART 7

A MOON'S BEGINNING 101

STREETLAMP SNOW FLOWERS 103

OH WHEN J WORE RED 104

BLOOD MOON OVER MURRAY 105

IT COMES YELLOW FULL 106

BROKEN ON MAYSVILLE 109

AT SUCH HOUR 110

CIRCLES 112

PART 8

FEIGNING MADNESS 113

WHERE 114

FOURTEEN AND BLOND WHISKERED 116

WAKING OF THE MALL 117

LAUGH AND THE WORLD 118

FLOOD 120

ABOUT THE AUTHOR .... b
BOOKS BY LEE PENNINGTON .... d
A NOTE ON THE ORIGIN OF SEGOVIA'S FINGERNAIL ..... f

ILLUSTRATIONS BY JILL BAKER

LATE SHOWS	13
THE WALLS SING	19
EMPTY LOCKET	31
IN DARKNESS	55
ON A BIRD CRASHING	69
HAITI REVISITED (1)	74
HAITI REVISITED (2(	75
HAITI REVISITED (3)	78
HAITI REVISITED (4)	79
LEDA'S BIRD	87
PERFECT CIRCLES	91
IT COMES YELLOW FULL	107
AT SUCH HOUR	111
LAUGH AND THE WORLD	119

PART 1

COUNTING GALAXIES

SEGOVIA'S FINGERNAIL

He flings music from strings
like spreading star seeds, fingers
counting galaxies in the quiet dark
of light barely beyond a candle range.

One man, mostly a shadow above a stool,
his foot invading a smaller one velvet red,
a guitar on his lap delicate like robin eggs,
releases stolen seeds which hang star planted
in walls like ancient odors
slipping from an open lid of a forgotten trunk.

The silence of thousands the deepest of all—
full like the great dark places in space.

Two together on the front row: he sits, hands
folded on his lap almost in final pose
without the coins on his eyes, head down
the sounds cover him like a comet's
tail always away from the sun; she
watches all, more than hearing—the
man, guitar, fingers, foot on red velvet;
the thousands still in breath-stopped silence;
her hands stroke the mink wrapped around shoulders
her own fingers feel the music of fur.

He doesn't see, but thinks he hears one lost note,
and sits wondering if such is the same
as words never spoken.

She sees it all, thinking maybe even
the hair-line crack before the strings ripping—
shooting it like a meteor to the front stage
where it lays shaped like a moon's beginning dark to full—
the haunting color of unmelting ice.

He thinks now the music will go with him always,
even to the grave, and even then perhaps
hover over the new mound of earth.

But she, long past hearing (if ever),
already sees it hanging on the wall
neatly framed with fingered gold
and a tiny brass plate saying "Segovia's Fingernail."

She knows she must have it
and quietly prepares to rush the stage
at the concert's end—
feigning madness on the floor.

MUSIC'S SPHERE

What must you do to earn
the night? Into song
stilled lengthy as lips of birds
frozen of light
nowhere in words
can such silence burn
lifting flames long
beyond ears of hear—
yet noise, constant fear.

What must you do to set
in motion music's sphere
a turning in a turn
a movement out of quiet?
Wings wave without devotion
to flight; songs clear
lie still as discarded white
snake skins (love's lament).
Precious the loss and yet
we have no time to forget.

POET LAYERS

Dreaming immortality more than gifted
stones, she wrote circles in her mind,
drew dark wonderful lines
outward—thoughts nearly spoken,
distant thunder promising rain
yet passing always east and west
of her nightmares.

Blank sheets were white fear enough
to coat fingernail lies under red.
Even words nearly made
rested desperately in her eyes
no rain could wash away.
What did others have to spring them clear,
what magic striking fire to thunder
splintering word beyond the burning?

She first ate seashells rubbed by the sea's
great belly against the earth—hoping the sound
of dragons would frighten words out
but all she craved of white silence
still lay under some red glow.
Then she gathered stones, searched
familiar faces born of ice and tumbling
and weather's other workings
but found such forms in the light
go dark in the dark.

Only one thing left if she could not touch
the word: touch the toucher and she ran
her dreams to sleep following every
moon wind down, spread her own mystery
to catch the dripping wild juice song.
And still after the singing all was not right
as her last lover opened up the night.

STANDING ON THE BANKS OF THE HUDSON
(For Allen Ginsberg)

I saw poets,
        the hudson river filled with their dots,
   their jazz,
their hair, bodies, slums, leaves and hopes
                                tied together,
this gyrating generation, by Eliot's lasso while
               Frost,

                       Sandburg,

                                Yeats
set in a sunburned west.

These were poets:
        water,
            stream,
                humps and rumps,
                        T.B. and T.V.
Their antennas of pragmatic stigmatism hunched psychoanalysis
and his chiropractor bones.
Whitman's blistered bubble burst good and juicy
                            and a million
gallons of them hung together like sewage dung.

The critics paddled out to the middle with their dung boats,
touching their screw finger to the water,
                    the poets,
                        standing

on the banks reeling for fish eggs.
                        Water   poets
                                water   poets
                                        water   poets
water, water, water enough to gag the stump of a horse
trying to hump a cow!

The critics kept goosing the ganders
                                trying
                                to get them to lay eggs!

Eggs they could crack for frying
                        soft shell
                                with lots of
                                        WHITES
        no
        yellow,

yellow is too sticky!   Too messy
                                it turns the plates
                                of future generations.
Good White Eggs, Good Slimy White, Non-Yellow
no plate Smearing Eggs of Ganders!

I saw a
        Bottle
                In the water, a single poet floating by. Hell
how the critics Howl!
                        Inside the bottle a broken egg with
Tons
        Gallons
                Quarts
                        Pints
                                Bushels
                                        Thimbles
                                                OF EGG YELLOW!

The bottle bobbed on the waves.
And the critics took after it in their dung boats,
                                                    their underwear
"Nities" (some hung below the cloth).
                                            They cried for poet help.
LET US BREAK THIS BOTTLE!!!!!!!!!!!!!!
The yellow splashed around the bottle.
Critics threw rocks,
                    tried to hit it with their dung oars,
                                    tried to kick it!
Poets chased too.
                    The bottle floated
                                on!
Some poets got too close and
                     the lid opened and
                          YELLOW
                    spilled out!
Hell oh hell how it hurt!
The yellow ran down their
        necks
                backs
                        eyeballs
                              ears
                                    noses
                                          teeth
                                                and
                                                      toenails.
The critics tried to lick it off before it stained
                    and found
their tongues coated.
                                                The bottle floated on.
The critics said
            "GOO
                    GOO
                            GOO"
                                        and their yellow tongues hung

farther
　　　d
　　　　o
　　　　　w
　　　　　　n
　　　　　　than their dongs.
And someone tried to find out what dong meant.
In Chinese it means to understand.

But the yellow critics
　　　　　　　　yellow tongued
　　　　　　　　　　　　　　yellow donged
Just stood there,
　　　　　　　and none of them did!

LATE SHOWS

I cup my hand to hear self
whispering over popcorn and 2 a.m.
t.v. upped commercial blur
& feel my words spit back into
My stung open mouth like
Finger-in-the-bottle spewed beer.

Getting up so I don't care if I have
20% fewer cavities or use poo poo
razor blades. Perhaps I'll skip the shave
come morning and cover up not showering
with after-lotion.

I've seen all the late shows
three times around anyway.
Why should I care if the sudden between
film blurb noises are louder
and keep waking me up
so I can choose whether I want to watch
what I've already seen and don't care
for anymore?

SHADOWS UNDER THE STONE
(In Memory of T.S. Eliot)

Down across the whirling sands
a shadow, wet with time, stands
alone without the man—
the planner of the plan.

Sweeney's lips cry out in the dark;
as dogs bedding, they circle, bark
then settle back around the cave
of mouth. They are slave
now to printed word.

Led by Valkyries
the creator slips into centuries.

The day
began as wasteland mushrooms
sprang from pits
like bats
and left the tombs
empty except for bleached crickets

beasts of unsunned cellars.
Now the greater pain of fallout.

Quietly in solid hesitation
the quake spins mind in reverberation
as dry as those white bones,
undershadows of stones.

Men hanging from their tongues taste
only the waste
of death.
Dry breath
rumbles again
out of season
and without reason:
no rain.

Listing as in waves rocking
like time ticking, clocking
broken hands around the face:
asteroids turn black in inner space.

Nightingales break bread
scratch in snow, are dead.

We shall crawl bone to bone
alone
often scattered together
as weather
somewhere wipes a hand across
the face of climate, of loss.

We shall crawl
like water dripping from thaw
of individual.

As snakes shedding skins
when year begins,
we shall crawl away on our bellies and back again
another year
and new skins will appear,
but the conditions of this frame
will never again be the same.

AMARETTO KISSES

The sun hunts its way down
trees thick as hands
where your gold necklace, bright
as fireflies, mirrors the nettle's
high sting of love.

I would say a woodpecker's cry
distant as unicorn clouds.
I would change places with clover blossoms
pressed in your heart's valley,
thinking too of the redbird's song.

Bernardino Luini knows a window's gift
and she immortalized in Saronno.

But the kisses, remembering almonds,
some sanctuary's fresco
heart hidden, weigh
what the world would weigh
without the night.

THE WALLS SING

Between walls claimed by cobwebs,
beside fly ghosts (a final buzzing)
sit
I my brown way into morning
drinking my mirror,
feet crossed to break the barefoot chill.

Walls speak that way (perhaps
it's singing). Long
lines creep
like old houses settling.

The crack by the fireplace
eases down to the baseboard, up to the ceiling.

I guess it a poem
carved from the awful stillness
of old wallpaper.

The Walls Sing — Jill Baker

PART 2

MOSTLY A SHADOW

DRAWING WATER

In the tall gray leather light of morning
fingers found trees against the sky
winter watch birds bursting air
crows crying out their sundays
the sun   drawing water   a unicorn
I have walked   waited   watched
time's turning   time's terrible twisting.

I have stood silent as old worts
waiting the wake   waking the wait
patient as secret promises never made
until up in the reaches of misery
too late cedar blooms yellow orange down
seeds fling fly to ice suspended
another year come around
wrapped in dishrags   buried
feed at last to startled chickens.

And oh the proud ripping corners of love
die in blood   songs of darkness
open liquid light. I am cyclops blinded
feeling bellies of sheep   hands tied
invisibly to a memory eye
If this cave be time's burned sphere.

THE HEART OF DOGHOWLS

In some dark distance

from the heart of doghowls

time clinches

a fist of hours

too full of wandering street

carrying songs almost born.

One crying whisper

one moment

hung on lips

red in the dying dawn.

The miles' quietness

waits everywhere

for roosters to crow.

The edges of every city

smell of night,

feel the weight

of hammer hearts

pounding silence.

THIS MORNING I WAS THIRTY

I rise with dawn, my 10,957 one,
and remember still last night's full moon
hanging above trees
and near shadow clouds slipping
like white lady slippers on spring.

This morning I was thirty;
my meat seems unchanged
since last night's one year ago.

My fingers stretch into morning
on green keys, too hard for grass,
too soft to be steel,
and I have seen my face
scattered brown with the grounds
in the bottom of nine empty cups.

So I have lived thirty springs and summers and autumns
and winters and have seen the red snow fall.
I've seen frost too early,
spring too late,
and winter lose by winning.

I've seen eyes, the dying roots,
stare from my generation
and I've watched a white cue ball
clicking others on green felt—
and laughed and cried
when the corner pockets sucked them in.

I've heard weeping of unborn children,
crying as they do on the ancient sky-is-falling legends
brought now all too real.

I have seen moons full enough in number
to make a calendar by themselves
and have gone searching, in that strange hour,
when the moon is dark and all silent.

I have seen stars fade out,
streak like bright raindrops down a window
and I have seen new ones come.

I have heard singing in the streets,
crying on the wind,
and at the distance I sometimes stand
they seem the same.

I have been told that I've done great things.
I have been told I have done nothing.
This morning it no longer matters.

This morning I was thirty
and I have watched the river go beyond trees,
I have seen the wind blow beyond roads,
I have hated and loved and lived and lied.
I have spilled sunlight
in the valley of the shadow
now five seasons gone.

Yet I will not look back into that shadow
nor ahead into the sun.
I will merely find my face in the cup bottom,
one more time,
the tenth time,
before morning is done.

FREEFALL RAIN

So we come to rainfall
contracted to sidewalk listening
of water trying to be glass
in a world where such and steel
are dreams trying to be
where rain begins.

Trying to be
is our age unlike Homer
on Trojan plains
with an oversized hobby horse
view beyond those blank caves.

Even if in freefall
the droplets, numbered only
by angels in the slums,
were not to explode
in hate of sun,
some child running
would dance
in such rhythm and heat
that clouds
would wring pretended hands
in agony and rage.

NIGHT THEY CALL IT

Night they call it
worms walked on in rain streets,
plump juice of pink
crushed grey or green,
and I stand by all the streetlamp stars
make wishes again
beside headlights blinking past.

City it is
though never called but on sirens
ringing red past puddles
making mirrors of mud
and ice cream
of children's fingers.

TO FILL AN EMPTY LOCKET

This:

Stare across time to some near thought. Strain
memory like pulling apart
Leaves of a book left out in the rain,
Try to read stuck together pages.

Know whispers that say everything, nothing,
in that frozen look, the ice of love,
laughter breaking away in glaciers.

Something black touching delicate flesh
Like the darkness inside the locket
Closed tight, a worship place.

When Cyclops enters that strange, sacred cave
unicorns at last lie down
in yes.

Empty Locket   Jill Baker

DOWN IN THE DUMP

He twists a hat
around his head;
it fits any position
like a rat.

There are others in the city's dump
with their bags and sticks, raking
in yesterday's rubbish for bread.

The sun wipes lips across the forgotten
who wade beside grey creatures.

Where do you go, old man?
Old woman?
Time got your tongue?
You know yesterday's manna is today's dung.

This rattle of tin cans
is man's
own echo,
I know—

I heard the last bird sing
I heard the last clock tick.
I heard the last of everything.
I hear the mouse trap click.

Don't give me that Joe's Bar stuff,
I know Charlie. He's like way
ahead of LSD or morning-glory seeds.
He's like a chewed piece of bubble gum.
Like a misfire, misfit. He's down

In the dump
Hunting tomorrow.

ALPHABETICAL

He said the A given a face

Looked like the Klan

and perhaps that's the way

it was meant to B,

don't you C?

Sort of D-day in the language,

E-z to comprehend

F you had a mind to,

G, I didn't know that

said one but makes an

H of a good story.

I didn't either said another.

Then the cry of the blue J

was A-O-K.

Maybe L-Camino Real.

The others chanted M

like songs TM lost,

Like doorknobless doors

and you can't get N.

O I C; mind your P & Q

if you only have one Q.

Yes, R something like that.

S-ince suits to a T,

U know that.

V-va stopping short

of W Shakespeare

who said X

was the end anyway and no reason Y

and we spend our final ZZZ's

A L P H A B E T I C A L L Y

I AM LOVED WITH SLABS OF SUNBURN

I am loved with slabs of sunburn
when chestnuts redden ripe for picking
and nerves stretch to rubber band apogee
toes cramp with unconscious thinking
the rhythm of bones and muscles set free.

I am loved with slabs of sunburn
burning bodies between pain and laughter
sea soaked in love, bandaged sea smelling
faster sometimes before sometimes after
the mandrake abrasive leaves the peel crawling.

I am loved with slabs of sunburn
tanned too soon flaked layers of cells
tanned too soon blistered white skin
the surface scoured with golf ball chills
parched water particles held within.

I am loved with slabs of sunburn
when the love-sun rises to peak of noon-day
when the stagnant shadow of self is lost
when no hot legs of time stand in the way
and katydids sing of a forty-day-away frost.

THE MAGICIAN'S REPLY

It hovers still over magic,
claims pictures lovely as words,
bursts every flower.

I have gone many more than counting time,
lifted it to cupped hands,
worshipped eternity's glimpse.

Yet, I am left with sensing lines
beyond Lilith.
I am left with breathing an odor
that remembers remembering.

Behind closed eyes I welcome an image
that will never know—
a magician's hands too quick,
a sorcerer's heart too slow.

REVERSE

Grey wings like whispers
on wind-paths tonight
are trails blazed
in shadow woven atmospheres
left
dancing white fanged screams.

The subtle land
is upside down
when dawn must be
to bats
a sunset.

BETWEEN THE STARS AND TREES

Between stars, trees and dawn
there is a moment when the last light
heaven sent and years come and the last
dark holding trees, all is one—
a time when no stars are, no trees.
The same light which makes trees
unmakes stars. The brightest
one last held. The smallest
tree last to show. Beyond day,
opposite—which is to say
arriving round between trees and stars
there is one time neither night nor day.

TIME'S VACANT PITS

Time stands Greek-bare-breasted
casting grey opposite the sun.
His eon's work is rested,
his sculpture is well done.

This is not an artist satisfied,
His rest is only a second
Blacked out and digested;
Ready at dawn with different hand

to chisel and carve another change
in his sculpture, his sepulcher.
His morning quest to rearrange
the sounds will only endure

long enough in the ear
to becomes echoes of memory:
black spots with dusty fear—
salt condensed from the sea

water and laid fresh on the beach
to dry, and for winds to blow
again to places out of reach.
We grasp moments but do not know

what mysteries they hold within.
Like vision of pressed lovers' lips
rocked back and forth and lost again,
aroma rises from the vacant pits.

PART 3

STOLEN SEEDS

ASCENSION

While morning slices under
the green edge of the moon
and leaves shake with birds
breaking glass stillness
with weighty dark,
I slip beside the rooster crow
walking a fence row of sound
down behind the Big O.

My hands become the surf
greeting piper dawn—
no, a crucifix of a man,
one hand the dying moon
the other the birthing sun,
shadows around my head
constant thorns.

Three days now in the tomb,
the rock rolled back,
rolled back.
I ascend beyond the bone
my spirit, now shadow, my clone.

PAGAN GODS

I carve gods in darker wood—
river faces that stare eternally
beyond places water
crawls away silently.

Gods emotionless as stone—
a look, position bound
a book, pages uncut,
deities with no sound.

Who will come after me
self-made such as these,
with less familiar blades
cut faces as they please?

MODERN GALILEE

The evening perked its ears,
lifted its nose from the trail of night,
returned, and proceeded to
waddle along toward the dusk.

At just the precise moment
before the earth's star disappeared,
the crosses shoved their shadows
as far as they could
and then flash-like
retraced their thin silent paths.

They never go anywhere;
only the shadows move about
and then only when car beams or
angled sun-light forces them.

Man guesses, by logic,
that shadows do not move in the dark.

Slaves of man are these crosses.
Also, a refuge for tired birds.
They stand erect, well creosoted,
and carry the voices of time along.

But why should man hear the voices?
Even the birds on the wires
feel nothing under their feet.

DISCIPLE DOVES

Above the easy silent green
nearly autumn on edge of leaves
twelve doves circle frantically
as if something terrible and strange
stalks the skyway of their range.
Searching where no rolled back stone
blocks their view, except clouds
grey with storm's intent, they build
a certain pattern then break away
in merriment and a hush of wind
clatters from their wings, brushes
back the dressy limbs.
Neither *V* nor *Cross* they carry
yet a nervousness,
a dust devil of feathers,
and night would be so kind
to let the day rise and follow
where the twelve have gone.

ROLLING SILENCE

Some say clover, some straw
when he crawled from Galilee
like an ant fallen from the line,
walking alone by the sea.

Some say blood, some tears
on poles crossed
like two fingers wishing
for something lost.

Some say light, some darkness
around the rock, the stone
like some rolling silence
gathering into moan.

4TH STREET

I stand downtown on Fourth Street
where shadows love the crowd's feet
more than sun. Brick stone eyes stare
from the tomb, city tomb, down where
I am, down on the knees of Fourth.
The city prays, for what it's worth,
here in red canyons of honking horns,
red lights stuck like a crown of thorns
between building sides. So I stand
on Fourth Street with a blind hand.

CREATION

We were down
among the reeds
and found
the last drink of paradise
was filled
with dregs.

We crawled
along the beach
like love
lost in breath
of moving whispers.

Sound caught
forever in the
acorn.

We, snapped from
the click
of time,
found only
sound.

Then
the moan
and creeping vines
saw sun,
dripped droplets
to the soul
of ground.

PARADOX

I am alone like a tree in the forest;
the wind all around me sings.
My branches move slowly with each bit of onthrust;
I am a follower of followers, a leader of kings.

The night wind bends gently the tip of my trunk.
My long roots tug harshly at earth,
and I am somewhere with a feeling defunct—
a seed grown mature three days before birth.

I have lived long in shortness of time.
My weak power from out lives within.
My blood condenses to cool solid lime.
and I finished in time to begin.

They slew me and burned me to clear for new land;
I flew through the air quick and free.
They buried my ashes in a river of sand
and knew I was not if I be.

WILDWOOD

We did not know it wise

to turn on the Wildwood Motel,

make it a house of love,

a tiny room we could easily fill,

crickets chirping outside,

a sink singing drops at a time,

a green wall where our

one hour martinizing covered clothes

could hang across from Jesus on the cross.

DAY LIGHT

I should have known
when I found five John the Baptist hogs
the day would long be out of reach
and I covered them still with weeds
while flies, green and otherwise
sang the dirge.

But no matter.
I've found favor anyway
with pagan gods
carved from wilderness
whose bright faces age back
to wood again as though
their carver has never been.

Getting lost in self I'd guess
is mud on boots
arms singing with nettle kiss
and four fireflies blinking in the day
a signaling the night they miss.

FISH SONGS

Out on grey streets rain slush
catches light faces, stains the near gold
to shadows, wet dirty film insisting
more night than cat howls in the distance.
Pools, caught like upside-down horses' hoofs
sing street songs of splashing flowers.
Sad songs turned on wheels churning
fog from dark valleys the size of a man's hand
or a man's mind tortured on turning
weather. Grey streets slush stained,
grey men blood stained, the clang
of a manhole opened to speak
forgotten fish songs.

IN DARKNESS

In darkness I have challenged
a moon's ripping,
slicing open edges of trees
curling around distant dog howls
laying waste fingers of love.

In darkness I have moved,
Silent as Indian heads fading on old nickels,
gone down to rivers beginning
ran nights mirror
through desperate hands.

In darkness I have claimed
songs of silence
searched the far reaches of whispers,
a rubbing of dried pine needles,
dreading the light.

In darkness I have stood
both dreamer and dream
embodied the curse
sensing full well dawn's drift
and what's even worse—
half knowing the universe.

In Darkness — Jill Baker

PART 4

THE GREAT DARK PLACES

IN THIS THE WORLD

In another jungle guns
explode.
Yellow flashes and blue smoke
fuse
to this green feeling now.
Bombs sprinkle the earth
Scattering man like the first rain
on sand. Only the sand
is already dead.
Exploding bombs and guns
(and all the screams
coming from mouths of unborn men)
all for the cause of death.

This morning I went down to the river
and stood throwing stones
into the dirty water, listened
to sounds. Later
took to weeds where no road
was broken. My ears heard
the tiny explosions
and face felt shrapnel.
Touch-me-nots with orange eyes
stared from the dark world.
Here explosion of weeds
All for the cause of life.

BAREFOOT WITHOUT THE GULLS

My eyes sweep the surf like low flying
gulls scooping up sand crabs,
soaring inches above the floating glass.
A mirror chases the dawn sky,
exactly as the scurrying ghost softshells,
sideways always white pinchers raised,
this morning without enemies.

RAW BACKWARDS

The heat drives it in
with or without wind.
It's left to fry the white
of the mind.
You can hear it swish out
like a blacksnake whip
burning through air
unleashing a sound of breaking bricks.
You hear it in the eyes
when they stone the children
and turn loose wild wolves
in the street.
Today they served
it to me for breakfast
smiling bloody
on a platter.

"WAR IS KIND"

Will you whimper when dust
dancing on your lips turns grey
in moldy moonlight and blinking
toads fling worts across your face?

Christ! I would rather be the underside
of snakes never able to see tops of grass
than go underground and have my screas
rolled into snowballs and flung back.

The witches of humanity
gather sage for brooms
which coil like cobras ready to strike
the wasting afternoon.

Will you still moan when they lower you
down and rake the sandy mound over
and leave you there beyond forever
in the wind and clover?

FLY BY NIGHT

Fly by night in this rain-soaked testimony
of time. Forgive them father for they know
what they do. They know the movement of wind,
the sound of breaking and young screams.
I have seen them smile and bow courteously
at some gutted child who hangs on the arms
of broken mothers, not his own for she
like the church is dead…dead…dead.

Today they worship their own private Jesus
and watch gentle wars add scar to scar,
scab to scab and play vampires
on other blood. This wet figbar
rolling in the paste, the waste—
in sand, and turned dirt to extended
hands and open mouths.

                    Today a child.
Yes, a child came to me and asked
what is red   and what is black
and I could not answer him. He asked
what is the color of blood and I could not.
He asked what is the color of gentle night,
Nothing. Daddy says we are Christ's crickets
chirping out his glory. We are pure
and white and he hugs our clean white bodies
to his wounds and we are pure and gentle.

Fly by night in this rain-soaked testimony,
Forgive them father for they know what they do.

THEY AND THEIR FATHERS

The one with the long gun
carries proudly
beside the one with the short gun
a robin clutched tightly in his tiny hand.

They carry baby guns—modeled
on their father's dream
of blue steel manhood.

Earlier, the other way,
they searched limbs now red
with October

They, how do you say it,
hunted birds
to bring down in blood—
theirs and their father's.

It was a great moment for him

(and his father).

Eyes bent slightly over the bead,

hands shaking, sights against the sky,

squeezing the trigger into death downward,

He does not know (nor does his father)

he tore a greater moment, forever,

from spring.

POLLUTION

Black cinder
screams blanket us,
smoke thoughts burn
our eyes. We've killed the wilderness,
no place now to turn

for hope clear winds
for touch soft rains.
The count too high
doesn't leave us much.

You know,
we've traded a blood sun for a day moon
and even that will be dark soon.

PART 5

COINS ON THE EYES

ON A BIRD CRASHING INTO A CLOSED WINDOW

From high in spring bursting
you swing down gathering speed till the world
you leave behind becomes the one ahead
and your image flashes before you,
closer and closer on yourself till
there is too much of you in front
coming quickly, too much to shift your downward
wings another way. You plunge into yourself
into total blackness.

Slamming glass at too much speed
you fling from flight torn from direction
of what must have seemed space was clear
steel which turned you into silence on the grass.
Now blood moments churn like bubbles rising
from boiling water, twist between clouded eyes,
put together a too sudden stopped flight
when your coming met full your going.

On a Bird Crashing
Into a Closed Window

Jill Baker

BLUE GILLS

A changing light releases
humming creatures (they roar
away fish-tailing others in the school).
But these have pilots, lured
through dense web entanglement
and then stretches of black, divided white
and yellow, outward in sun waves.
These are intelligent beings, not
from another world but hard set
to there. These are sea creatures
sea smelling salt singing Vikings of another order.
Rushing, pushing, pressing, mashing
their way forward, waving to turn
to pass—bait awaited unwarned blue-gills.
They blow blue sound bubbles; they stare
in one direction, straight lined beams
in rhythm: BRIGHT dim, BRIGHT dim, BRIGHT dim, BRIGHT!

Along the bank stands the fisherman
dark clothed, giant-scythe-like fishing rod.
He casts right into them then slowly
brings across his tantalizing fly.

The blue-gills (hungry, proud or curious)
play in close, play asleep and unconcerned.
Then one bites. Then another. And another. Another.
And big wheel, little wheel blue-gills
(skinned, boned, beheaded) are ready
For the fisherman's frying pan.

HAITI REVISITED
(Or: What is the Color of a Negro's Ghost?)

In the presence
of all time:
you do not remember?
In all the rain and the flashing?
There was a question that night.
Now on another dark of the world
there is still the question.

Spectra rises from catacombs,
fifty-thousand sand-sought souls
prepare the macabre;
Haiti trembles, rumbles.

Malodorous incense rises from pits,
smoldering blue gangrenous creatures
slither from succulent earth slits.
The tremor awakes all.
Gehenna gathers her futurity; the necrology is read.
"UMBER, EBONY, SIENNA, SEPIA!"
Let the dance begin!

Aboriginal sculptures
dry the wet vermillion fog
from bronze lips
then each to his own eats madder.

Curly hair, wooly hair.
Broad nose, flat nose
Snapping brown-black eyes.
Epicanthic folds.
Prognathism.

The ocher, sweaty spirits
drink verdancy.

One by one
the spirits prepare to speak:
GHOST
SPECTRE
GESPENST
SPETTRO
FANTASMA
SPOKE
GAYST

GHOST: You, Sir, once I saw you, me thinks.
               It was in Alexandria, and you came late,
               stood
               and
               watched.
               I believe I saw you that day?

Haiti Revisited — Jill Baker

Haiti Revisited

GESPENST: Hakenkreuz!

GHOST: Do I remember your hair?
            Sir, will you not speak?

SPECTRA: (Pedant) l'apres midi
            je chanterais,
            Voulez-vous du pain?

            Il y a repondu
            Donnez le livre

GHOST: Son of man know you not
            the purpose of stone?
            Know you not the rust
            of skin? The weathered iron?

GESPENST: Am Morgen,
            Ich Verstehe.
            Am Abend,
            Ich Verstehe nicht.

GHOST: Yours are eyes from empty skulls.
            In the dark of broken bones
            the blue corpse waited for
            the dark wood to collapse.

SPRETTO: Scusi
           Non Parlo.
           Buona notte.

GHOST: To die is such motion
           of snakes crawling through
           the empty white bones
           in the black earth.

FANTASMA: Hace mucho que estoy aqui.
           Hay mucha gente aqui,
           Hay nuebla, tener sed,
           tener miedo.
           tener prisa,
                  tener razon
                  tener la culpa!
           El hombre muerto temio que el enemigo
           Le hubierse oido.
           Los jovenes tenien que limpiarse las manos

GHOST: White piano keys dance with blackness,
           Pink bottom hands thrill trumpets.
           Inside that dark room. The snake pit
           of our souls; the forked tongue
           licked the meat from our faces.

SPOKE: forkyla sig
           kanna sig
           lara sig
           Saga man will. Jag tror!

Haiti Revisited — Jill Baker

Haiti Revisited — Jill Baker

GHOST: You could not hear our bones
until the meat was gone.

SPOKE: At vilket hall ar norr?
At vilket hall ar soder?

GHOST: Brother of dragons,
companion of owls,
My skin, too, is black upon me.
My bones, too, burn with meat.

GAYST: Ver iz duss?
Vemen zet er?

GHOST: The wind goes toward the South
and turns about in the North.
It whirls continually and the wind returns.
Dead flies in the water of the sun.
Into the darkness were we driven
till our shadows curled like dust
over our bodies and the shadow
of a great stone was on a weary land.

GAYST: Ikh hob moyre!

GHOST: In the City of Fog, near the pit,
we came dripping with flesh.
In the Kingdom of Darkness
we knew the great whore and
the worms of the earth
crawled through her black mystery.

LIST OF THE DEAD

Sky bound, shattered,
    read black on white
    bodoni type
list of names, mattered
only to souls splattered
airborne, missing flight.

Head wind, broken
    winged, dust damp
    ice bloods stamp
thoughts unspoken,
no thanatopsis token,
headless hobo tramp.

Headlined, enough said,
    Wreckage twisted
    tabulated,
downed, unsought dread
gangrene hopes instead
all listed, all dead.

FAR CRY FROM ENEMY

Gulls patter in damp wind, restless as boarder
sand grains.
Tracks made are covered, made again.
Water hisses like grass snakes pumping.
"Go away!" Water hissing. Gulls throb
Melodrama.
"Don't get too close now! Hear?" Hissing and throbbing.
"Come back away before the old boogie man gets you!"
Hissing.
Restless pattering in damp wind,
tracking up the clean, damp sand.
Endless, restless sand. . . wind. . . boogie man. Hissing!

PART 6

MUSIC OF FUR

THE SEA OF MY FINGERS

You need not fear the sea of my fingers.
You forget, I have made love with the moon
in every wilderness bed, in every darkwood.
I have gone while storms rage (night's
 own lover), when she hides like breath shadows,
found her in green moss
or standing behind the glass of rivers.
I have mounted the moon, like a wild stallion,
singing to her while she stood for me
taking me in till I am her madness.

THE WHITE WOLF OF YOUR EYES

The white wolf gathers light
Whispers warm coming beyond
silence, stillness beyond saying,
need beyond knowing.

Cool like corners
of moonlight touching stones
silver, scattering darkness
searching the night.

Maybe Orpheus water,
Gatherer of intoxicating dew,
you hummingbird kiss
the honeysuckle nectar.

Know I am the sound
nearly made, earthbound stone,
and the light's last sweetness
hangs in the flower's bone.

LEDA'S BIRD

Dark wishes stain the night
spill softly down near
silence of old wood. A voice
open flame wine wind bleeding rain.

Beyond shadow snakes crawl
listening with their tongues
to your songs of honey fingers.

Were I to worship wisdom I would
first hold the truth of your eyes
suspended like smoke in winter chill
curled around the promise of rain
no less than Leda's bird
white as snow in love's dance.

Your eyes move, your shadows away,
you capture the bird in trance.

Ledo's Bird — Jill Baker

APHRODITE WELCOMES NIGHT

More than red scattered or gold gentle
your own frenzied love whispers fire
trembling toward darkly December limbs;
waves sweep your mirror to silence.

Singing the yes
of your eyes' dreams,

lost in pools –
shadows deep blue
delicate as butterfly breath,

you touch the silence silver
of siren songs.

The sun, mysteriously yours,
catches the horizon.

PERFECT CIRCLES

Your lips, perfect circles,
wake the morning of my face
like hearing secret music
spilled from earth –

I mean the way water
runs down deep in stone,
the way there are rivers
never seen but flowing

always around and around
without a sky, a dawn,
and blind fish swim
an arc coming, going forever

passing where they've been
yet new, dark, wonderful.
My tongue one, breaks to enter,
all of you concentric.

SEGOVIA'S FINGERNAIL

Perfect Circles   Jill Baker

CLINGING TO SEAWEEDS

I will the yellow down, first look
then touch, hands swim
around you like flowers, lips
taste raindrops bodies claim.

We are circling smoke, fire and flame
nudged wet by night's tears.
We are mirrored in cat eyes
clinging to seaweeds inside water.

We wake memory bursting time,
spill whisper dripping rivers.
Winds all around, the sirens sing
one moment lost of everything.

EVEN THEN

Even then
you said we must keep
the relationship Platonic
all this
as I unfastened your bra
and found proper dialogue
with my fingers.

Even then
you smiled light wise
and leaned to touch
your lips far away from mine,
on my forehead,
placing both of us
closer to logical
conclusion.

Even then
you said Platonic
in a wet whisper
tugging at my belt
as nylon, frail as hemlock,
curled on the floor.

Even then
we might have made it
had not your gifted hand
guided surely to Plato's
dark cave,

even then
Platonic.

SILENT FISH

I lie soaked in you
a perfect wetness
knowing all your waters

and sense sun on fog
giving light to both sides
if smoke has sides.

I carry you
circled by water.

Inside silent fish
happy as air
swim through you.

Beyond, yet near,
a lake and swans
and, yes, cattails.

The rains, my storms,
into your sea,
your waves rocking
under me.

THE HOMELY GOLD HAIR GIRL
AT THE FOOT OF THE STAIR

The homely gold hair girl at the foot of the stair
with thoughts as wide as saucer moons
tempts dawn with ready laughter
threatens every thunder storm with eyes
walks wavy like a winded willow
leaves footprints dandelion and daisy wise.

The homely gold hair girl collects bird songs
in her throat, births a troubled river
in her hands, locks the wolf cries in her heart.
She pretty sings the smoke skyward kite
and ribbons darty tailed in the wind
whisper rainbows into candlelight.

The homely gold hair girl, a wake of sun,
a wave of water waiting at the crest,
a dogwood red each petal christ tipped blood,
a mandrake straining apple yellow bloom,
wild ginger spice she, around the darker wood,
searches out the corners of earth's room.

THE BLUE GIRL

The blue girl sun dances
warm laughter, coloring the fog
her color, chasing fleecy clouds away
with her looking, and the early
spider webs of dawn reflect her doing.

The blue girl bathes in butterflies
stirring songs from shadows
splashing away the night
dripping with love
where water wings slip by.

The blue girl wakes the silence
melts the dark waiting
trembles spring into flowers
makes mirrors beyond the glass
and love sounds wait their turn
whispering the blue girl yes.

NO GOLF PERMITTED HERE

No golf permitted here nor love—
the browning grass beside lush green
frightened to life by angry water,
the parcourse trail closer now to nature
than to made, wild tennis courts
caged in else they get away.

No golf permitted here nor love—
who dreams such signs to make
us think those thoughts we've never thought,
do those things we've never dreamed?
Or is it merely given space,
without the signs,
golfers drive and lovers love
and warnings come later?

No golf permitted here nor love.
You can tell they've been here,
golfers and lovers,
a million staring white eyes
the grass's pressed down places,
and imagine each dark, each night,
glorious missiles set in flight.

BURDEN

The burden of grass
(to weigh the wind)
presses whisper down
damp in morning chill.

Folded like memory autumn
the brown steals green.
The night limps on light crutches
of broken stars, crippled space.

The burden of love holding
your green face, your lips
about to speak, your eyes
already Molly Bloom.

THE RAIN WOMAN WALKS

The rain woman walks barefoot
through the dripping woods
green with love
teaching birds to sing
touching buds to bloom
tasting red-white candy laughter.

The rain woman walks barefoot
pressing love downward
proving delight earthward as foxfire
willing dreams to waking
a whisper white as flowers
the color of angel wings.

The rain woman walks barefoot
roots reach out limbs reach up
fish, silent as eyes, slip
warm as hands through the water
and the hands have eyes
locking the vision into song.

PART 7

A MOON'S BEGINNING

STREETLAMP SNOW FLOWERS

They bloom at dusk, close at dawn,

Never opening at light's favor

But indigenous to the dark

Like so many things we never to speak about—

the chill and silence of the heart

the mind's broken lips

the weeping fingers of the moon

and how many bugs die a windshield death.

Automatic, even as our dreams,

given any night they bloom—

quiet as a severed rabbit's foot

on a key chain.

But the best is on the snow,

the corpse of rain,

their being spread evenly and down

and as if by petal fall

tracks leading up to

away from.

OH WHEN J WORE RED

Oh when J wore red
my eyes rivers
ran downstream
in a sea of sunsets

Oh when J wore red
her own eyes above
high cloudless skies
as if the autumn love
call of birds
wrote wingless words.

Oh when J wore red
I heard Columbus
white sail speak
first landing learn
Indians welcoming
the gods return.

Oh when J wore red
I, Balboa, tranced in view
a sight too immense
to grasp the new.

Oh when J wore red
I surely knew
all explorer's intent—
such stranding of dreams
fresh hovering a continent.

BLOOD MOON OVER MURRAY

Blood moon over Murray
one night after full
and I stand
with the head on the grass
for you, but your night fingers
feel my face
red with the dripping.

A yellow-haired moon
hot now to redness
hangs over the buildings,
over the hot streets
over my standing
and a child cries
in the streets being born.

Blood moon over Murray
where hearts sleep
on the sound of cotton
and eyes lick up
the stillness,
the silentness
of the red night no
wind sound.

IT COMES YELLOW FULL

The moon falls yellow full on hemlocks
and down like a woman's hair
where my eyes eat the meadow mist,
where my flesh leans against
the silence. I have listened for all
night sounds, and they wept like
crickets, but now they, too, are gone,
all except worms in love, their pink
bodies swollen on each till a footstep
drives them back to earth alone.
I touch the grass and wildberry
blooms. So I am tonight to know
the moon comes full, and her
hair falls yellow on the in heat meadow.

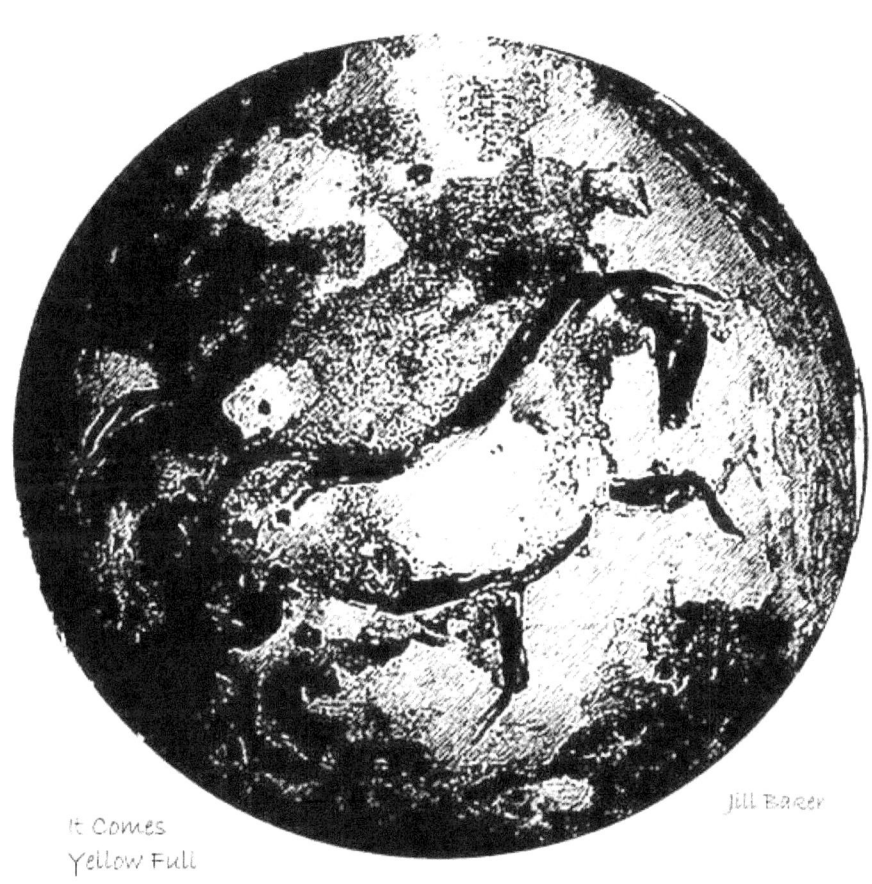

It Comes
Yellow Full

Jill Baker

BROKEN ON MAYSVILLE

The full fades yellow
soft like distant whispers
where light clings in stone hallways
soaking up silence.

To dare dark sculptures
carved from shadows burning with foxfire,
welcomes night frosty chill of love,
a snow awakening, a moon's dying
startles dreams deep as white wonder.

Beyond broken moments
hands hold secrets, gifted in pain and memory,
desire's fragments of the great
golden bird where dawn drifts, covers
all the grey spilled pieces of night.

Still the fingers claim yellow stain
torn from old butterfly wings
a moon's breath from love

and the heart's longing
is white wall reflection,
blood's water crystal fall.

A primal scream beyond the door
leaves arms empty of their hold,
sings another snow of winter cold.

AT SUCH HOUR

I have watched the trees shed the dark
slipping away like eyelids of birds waking,
lifting to stare, blind leaving, limbs stark,
vision coming slowly, caught and waiting, taking
sight cautiously, as if too much, too much light.
would turn it back again toward the night.

I have watched the morning give back the city
held so long in vapor amber flow, turning
thoughts, fog unnatural, air cinders black, gritty;
sidewalk beds, street men, arise to hearts burning,
seeing pigeons (urban doves) lift to flight
clipping the cloth horizon beyond their sight.

I have watched for evidence of wind
coming at such hour it, too, must awake
the whisper ice, crystal dreams, when wires bend;
casting moans aside, tall buildings shake,
empty bottle the sun's face, mirror, mirror plight—
tattered Pandora coats closed, held tight.

At Such Hour

CIRCLES

Dark you talk, as night clicks,
some light quicks, shadows tight as drum
chase black lace beyond horizon dead.
What was said need not be thought.

Noon comes soon, as if by ship;
winds sly slip around river bends.
Load the road, eternity's working feet,
where we meet fire, earth, water, air.

Now, somehow, we hear circles
coil fear, concentrically spoil
grief as thief, and if change be right
strange night has come around to light.

PART 8

FEIGNING MADNESS

WHERE

Who has lived the
blood of wheels—
each spoke a vein
on which life
hangs
like a cat
trying to cross
a crowded road.

I have been here
in sun and rain
on both sides of the tracks—
the dying sounds of trains
and alley screams
where the macabre
performs nightly dance
      and men
cheer
with the god, Profane.

The sun burns hotter here

and the snow melts slower

and men fly

like vultures

with distance

their prey.

FOURTEEN AND BLOND WHISKERED

You cannot, I tried, fourteen and blond whiskered.
A bitch in heat ran down the road leaving
liquor smells in the dust. The curs and I followed.
Oh how it hurt! We wore the bottoms off
our feet frenching the ground in four-four rhythm.
A dozen of us, our teeth shined. The fur raised
ropes for the red hoosegow knots like broken blisters.
Someone growled the pack into frenzy cut-throat;
one eye on the bitch and other on wounds,
we were the big boys licking it out to the limits.
Somehow between broken legs, split ears and death we lost.
Off to the side a smaller pup waged a wetter war and won.

WAKING OF THE MALL

The mall wakes on slow feet
crawling behind bamboo brooms, sweeping
scratching sounds into silence.
Clicking, cracking until motion
is river smooth over tile stones.
Forms become faces, windows
eyes, ash trays flowers; smoke
vines blue around silver air,
grows shimmering leaves,
and all voices become jungle manna
whisper tiger feet,
feeling the ivory
in lost elephant graveyards.
Off in the banyan shadows of mind
a hyena cries.

LAUGH AND THE WORLD

Laugh and the world at some blue skin buck,
grey with the whisper of evening, jack-knifed
and puking the stomach lining of terpentine,
shoepolish or goofjuices unalkalized, unseltzered,
in streets near the sanguine scent of policemen
billyclubs, twirling in the distant darkness.

Laugh and the world at awkward April crawling leopard
like over winter-raped buds with her red shiny eye.
Laugh and the world at souls of street, hair—
Trembling bodies laid naked for the nymphomania.

Laugh and the world at three men in a tub:
the butcher with his greasy gold cleaver,
carving meats; the baker browning his bread
too soon; and the candlestick maker
lighting blaze, eternally ember, at the mausoleum.

Laugh and the world like hieroglyphic hyenas
at green-black bellies of babies, oversized
and underfed while the hot-tailed prioress flings
her fur at hounds of heaven who come sniffing
the bitch-scent trail to warm their midnight stumps.

Laugh and the world at tombstones licking
convulsively the marching ants, crushed to shoe rhythm
of morning Valkyries. Laugh at vengeance of vacuum,
rigor mortis returning ripe down the staircases.

FLOOD

The bright blue is gone
fallen from the sky, wringing hands
twisting the rag, dripping the darkness
into storm.

Winds blow on the great mountain
tugging at trees
tearing at roots
throwing off leaves ripe with autumn.

And they come
elite in their cars
bound in their buses
high asses on their cycles
to spread love-hate in the morning.

They come to weep together
crying great tears in their beards
washing away the distance.

They come like sleepy cats
torn in their misery
between trips
to gift honor and love
to hold each other in each other
begging for space
on the forgiven planet.

They come on the wires
to cry of stealing.
They come on the water
barefoot and sandal dipped
in mercy and magnificence.

And they talk of injustice
like eating crackers
and coughing great white flakes
in the eyes.

They strip the mind
then go to save the land.
They piss burnt hate
then go to save the water
They cough cracker crumbs
then beg for air.

Then they fight
standing on the fingers.
Then they spin their eyes
like galaxies
sucking up firstborn land
nailing the love to tree limbs.

And down with the rednecks
down with the white asses
down with the black bastards
down with the goddamn rain
down with time which turns
dry streams to flowing
for now there is water
there is too much rowing.

ABOUT THE AUTHOR

LEE PENNINGTON is the author of 23 books, including *I Knew a Woman* (1977), *Thigmotropism* (1993) and *Appalachian Newground* (2016), each nominated for a Pulitzer Prize in poetry. His latest book is *Daughters of Leda* (2017). He has had over 1300 poems published in more than 300 magazines in America and abroad. He has had nine plays produced, wrote the script for *The Moonshine War* (MGM, 1970, starring Alan Alda, Richard Widmark, etc.), and has published thousands of articles and short stories in everything from *Playgirl* to *Mountain Life and Work*.

Beginning in 1990, through his video production company, JoLe Productions (joleproductions.com), Lee, along with his late wife, Joy, produced 21 documentaries, including *In Search of the Mudmen* (1990), *Wales: History in Bondage* (1995), and *Secrets of the Stones* (1998), *Eyes that Look at the Sky: The Mystery of Easter Island* (2001), *The Mound Builders* (2001), *The Serpent Fort: Solving the Mystery of Fort Mountain, Georgia* (2005), *Let Me Not Drown on the Waters: Fred Rydholm, Michigan's "Mr. Copper."*

Since Joy's death in 2011, Lee has produced five more documentaries: *Some Days You Clean, Some Days You Litter: The Amazing Warner Sizemore* (2012), *Room to Fly: Anne Caudill's Album* (2013), *Bosnian Pyramids: Hidden History* (2015), *Seafaring Strangers: Viking in America, Part I* (2016), and *Gunung Padang: Monument to Atlantis* (2017).

Lee is a graduate of Berea College in Kentucky and the University of Iowa. He holds two Honorary Doctor degrees: Doctor of Literature from World University, and Doctor of Philosophy in Arts from the Academy of Southern Arts and Letters. He taught for nearly 40 years, the last 32 as Professor of English and creative writing at University of Kentucky Jefferson Community College, until he retired in 1999.

He has traveled extensively in all the United States, all the Canadian Provinces, except one, and in 92 foreign countries. For the past dozen years he has served as president of the Ancient Kentucke Historical Association, a group dedicated to the study and research of pre-Columbian contact in the Americas.

In 2013 the University of Louisville opened the *Lee and Joy Pennington Cultural Heritage Gallery*, named after Lee and his late wife. The gallery contains U of L's most valuable works, including the likes of first editions of Galileo, Copernicus, and Newton. It will house all of Lee's writings and many artifacts he has collected traveling around the world.

He presently lives in Kratz House, a designated historic home in Middletown, Kentucky with his lady, Jill Baker, an artist who has illustrated several of his books.

BOOKS BY LEE PENNINGTON

The Dark Hills of Jesse Stuart (criticism), 1967

Scenes from a Southern Road (poetry), 1969.

Poems and Prints (poetry), 1969.

Wildflower...Poems for Joy (poetry), 1970.

April Poems (poetry), 1971.

Appalachia, My Sorrow (drama), 1971.

Songs of Blood Harlan (poetry), 1975, reprinted hardback 2019.

Spring of Violets (poetry), 1976.

Coalmine (drama), 1976.

The Porch (drama), 1976.

The Spirit of Poor Fork (drama), 1976.

Creative Composition (textbook), 1976.

I Knew a Woman (poetry), 1977, reprinted in 2018.

Ragweed (drama), 1980.

The Janus Collection (poetry/photography), 1982.

Foxwind (drama), 1984.

Appalachian Quartet (drama), 1984.

The Scotian Women (drama), 1984.

Thigmotropism (poetry), 1993.

Appalachian Newground (poetry, drama, essay) 2016.

Daughters of Leda (poetry), 2017

I Knew a Woman (poetry), Reprint, 2018

Songs of Bloody Harlan, first hardback edition, 2019.

A NOTE ON THE ORIGIN OF SEGOVIA'S FINGERNAIL

When I transferred to Berea College in the spring of 1958, I immediately was named news editor of the *Pinnacle*, the student newspaper at Berea. I had previously been sports editor of Baldwin Wallace College's *Exponent*, their student newspaper.

I was a second semester freshman at Berea, and with way more naiveté than I needed, when the editor of the *Pinnacle* asked me to go to Boone Tavern and interview a musician who was going to give a concert at the college.

You need to understand my background. I grew up in the head of a holler in Greenup County, KY and what I knew about the world probably would have fit fairly easily in our water bucket. I had never heard of Andre Segovia and simply had no idea he was already recognized, even in the fifties, as the world's greatest guitarist.

I knocked on his hotel door and said, "Mr. Segovia, I'd like to come in and interview you."

He invited me in and for the next four hours politely answered all my questions and even permitted this mountain boy an indiscretion I cannot imagine now. Even to this day, I carry some embarrassment when I think about it.

On the floor, in an open case, was one of the two hand-made guitars that had been made exclusively for Segovia in Spain. One he carried in a case on tours and the other he kept in a vault in Spain. He said he could not tell the two guitars apart when he played them.

Not even thinking, I looked at Segovia and asked, "Would you mind if I play your guitar?" I cringe even now, these 61 years later, of having asked that question.

This gracious gentleman, without any hesitation, said, "Go ahead."

I am certain, or fairly certain anyway, that it was the only time that "Wildwood Flower" was ever played on Andre Segovia's guitar! What I am even more certain of is that this mountain boy stood before a musical genius and received an act of kindness when that boy's own innocence opened the moment to such an unexpected gift.

Segovia played in Carnegie Hall in NY to sell-out audiences—people paying $10 a seat. At Berea College, when Segovia performed in the Phelps Stokes Chapel, we students paid 35 cents to hear him. It was the most amazing concert I have ever witnessed.

Gladys Jamison, a music teacher at the college, provided Segovia with a little red velvet covered stool to rest his foot on. With his guitar on his lap, and to a standing room only crowd in Phelps Stokes (the auditorium seats 1,200!), with no amplification whatsoever, Segovia held us spell bound for a very long concert—well over two hours. As I remember, there were nine standing ovation encores.

Norris Woody, a theology teacher and a very fine guitarist himself, was seen the next morning stuffing his own guitar in the trash can.

The memory of my encounter with Segovia was indelible.

Years later, I was thinking about that concert—what it meant to music, what it meant to art in general, what it meant to all of us, and I came up with the idea for the poem

"Segovia's Fingernail." I wanted to tell about two kinds of people—one who was totally immersed in art, and another who merely wanted to be seen at artsy things.

Then the idea grew. Thus, *Segovia's Fingernail*, the book, was born.